GET READ
FOR MINOR SCALE DUETS!

by Wynn-Anne Rossi and Victoria McArthur

Check Off (✓) when completed successfully with duet

Patterns for Success

There are three possible ways to play the scale duets (student primo part) in this book.

1. Many students and teachers will choose the *two-octave (parallel motion) version*, which is notated throughout the book in every key.

2. If you are just beginning your study of minor scales, you and your teacher may choose the *one-octave version*. This is not written out throughout the book, so you will need to memorize the pattern in order to play it in the keys which you will learn. This is not difficult if you notice how many times you will play the scale. A sample is included on this page in the key of A minor.

ONE-OCTAVE VERSION

To be played either hands separately or hands together, in any key.
Notice that the student part (primo) starts on measure 3 of the teacher part (secondo).

3. The most challenging version is the *two-octave (contrary motion) version*. It is identical to the two-octave (parallel motion) version written throughout the book, except for measures 13 – 16, which are different. Below is a sample in the key of A minor.

TWO-OCTAVE VERSION (CONTRARY MOTION)

To be played either hands separately or hands together, in any key.
Notice that the student part (primo) starts on measure 3 of the teacher part (secondo).

A Minor Snake Charmer

Secondo

adapted by W. Rossi

A Minor Snake Charmer

Primo

Funeral March in E Minor

Secondo

adapted by W. Rossi

Funeral March in E Minor

Primo

B Minor for Baroque

Secondo

W. Rossi

B Minor for Baroque

Primo

F♯ Minor Ostinato

Secondo

W. Rossi

F♯ Minor Ostinato

Primo

Native in C♯ Minor

Secondo

W. Rossi

Native in C# Minor

Primo

Romance in G♯ Minor

Secondo

W. Rossi

Romance in G♯ Minor

Primo

Invention in D Minor

Secondo

adapted by W. Rossi

Invention in D Minor

Primo

Irish Jig in G Minor

Secondo

W. Rossi

Irish Jig in G Minor

Primo

Caravan in C Minor

Secondo

W. Rossi

Caravan in C Minor

Primo

Hush-a-bye in F Minor

Secondo

adapted by W. Rossi

Hush-a-bye in F Minor

Primo

B♭ Minor Blues

Secondo

W. Rossi

B♭ Minor Blues

Primo

In the Hall of E♭ Minor

Secondo

adapted by W. Rossi

In the Hall of E♭ Minor

Primo

Getting to Know Close Relatives

Relative Minor

Every major scale has a relative minor scale, just as every minor scale has a relative major scale. Relative major and minor scales *share the same key signature*. Any of the three forms of minor can be a relative minor scale (see p. 29).

There are two ways to find the relative minor:

1. Start on the 6th note of the major scale. That is the relative minor name.

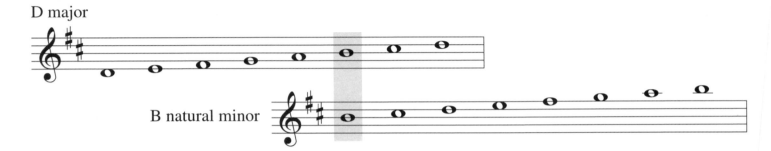

2. Start on the note three half steps below the major scale name. That also is the same relative minor name.

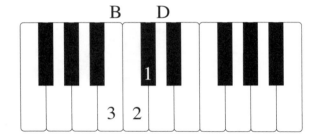

Parallel Minor

Parallel minor is different from relative minor. Parallel major and minor scales *have the same key names*, such as C major and C minor. Notice that parallel major and minor scales *do not* share the same key signature.

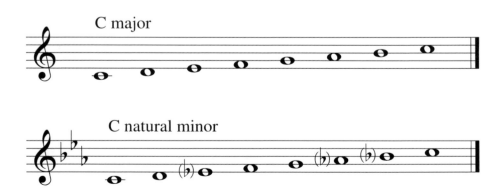

Scale Facts

Every major scale has a relative minor scale, which may appear in any one of three forms: *natural, harmonic,* or *melodic.* (See page 28 for a discussion of relative minor.)

- **Natural minor scales** all follow this pattern of whole and half steps.

  W H W W H W W

  It is also helpful to think of natural minor as the unaltered relative minor scale.

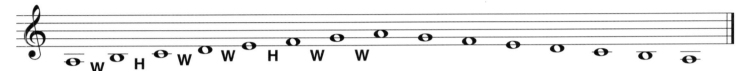

- **Harmonic minor scales** all follow this pattern of whole and half steps.

  W H W W H W+H H   *Notice the W+H, which is the characteristic feature of harmonic minor.*

  An easy way to remember harmonic minor is to *raise the 7th note* of a natural minor scale one half step.

- **Melodic minor scales** all follow this pattern of whole and half steps.

  W H W W W W H   **W W H W W H W**
  ascending   *descending*

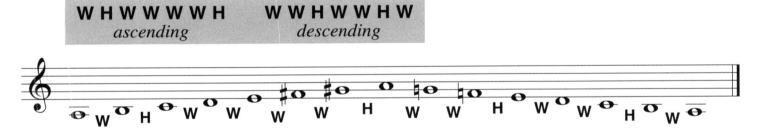

Notice that melodic minor is different from the other two forms of minor, since there is one pattern for ascending (going up), and another one for descending (going down). The descending pattern is a natural minor scale.

An easy way to remember melodic minor is to *raise the 6th and 7th notes* of a natural minor scale one half step when ascending, then *lower the 6th and 7th notes* when descending.

Feeling Sharp in a Minor Way!

There is an easy way to figure out the number and names of the sharps in each scale's key signature. Study the chart below as you learn each sharp minor scale.

Minor Key Name	Major Key Name	Number of Sharps	Names of Sharps
a	C	0 sharps	None
e	G	1 sharp	F♯
b	D	2 sharps	F♯, C♯
f♯	A	3 sharps	F♯, C♯, G♯
c♯	E	4 sharps	F♯, C♯, G♯, D♯
g♯	B	5 sharps	F♯, C♯, G♯, D♯, A♯
d♯	F♯	6 sharps	F♯, C♯, G♯, D♯, A♯, E♯
a♯	C♯	7 sharps	F♯, C♯, G♯, D♯, A♯, E♯, B♯

Notice that each sharp minor scale name is the interval of a 5th apart. Starting with the key of A minor (0 sharps), **move up to the 5th note** of that scale which is E minor (1 sharp, F♯). Then, **move up to the 5th note** of the E minor scale, which is B, and so on. Sometimes this pattern of moving by 5ths is called the Circle of Fifths.

Minor Flat-tery!

The flat scales, like the sharp scales, follow an easy pattern.
Can you figure out the pattern on your own after looking at the chart below?

Minor Key Name	Major Key Name	Number of Flats	Names of Flats
a	C	0 flats	None
d	F	1 flat	B♭
g	B♭	2 flats	B♭, E♭
c	E♭	3 flats	B♭, E♭, A♭
f	A♭	4 flats	B♭, E♭, A♭, D♭
b♭	D♭	5 flats	B♭, E♭, A♭, D♭, G♭
e♭	G♭	6 flats	B♭, E♭, A♭, D♭, G♭, C♭
a♭	C♭	7 flats	B♭, E♭, A♭, D♭, G♭, C♭, F♭

Notice that the flat scales are also a 5th apart, but this time you **move down by 5ths** (easy to remember since flat means to "move down"). Starting with the key of A minor (0 flats), move down a 5th to D minor (1 flat, B♭). Then move down a 5th for G minor (2 flats, B♭ and E♭), and so on.

Notice that the names of the flats themselves are also 5ths apart. The first flat in any scale is B♭. Move down a 5th to find the next flat (E♭), then A♭, and so on.

The Minor Scale Expedition

Now let's see how well you understand what you've read as you explore the territories
of the missing notes for each of the scales below. Notice that you will need to use each
letter in the music alphabet only once when spelling the notes of a scale. Award yourself
2 points if you get the correct answer all by yourself. Award yourself **1 point** if you get
the correct answer, but have to look it up. (The answers are listed at the bottom of the page.)

Points (1 or 2)

1. Starting on A, the next note in the natural minor scale is ____. _____

2. Starting on E, the next note in the harmonic minor scale is ____. _____

3. Starting on B, the next note in the *ascending* melodic minor scale is ____. _____

4. The notes in the F♯ natural minor scale are F♯, ___, ___, B, C♯, D, ___, F♯. _____

5. The notes in the *ascending* C melodic minor scale are C, D, E♭, F, G, ___, ___, C. _____

6. The notes in the *descending* G♯ melodic minor scale are ___, F♯, E, ___, ___, B, ___, G♯. _____

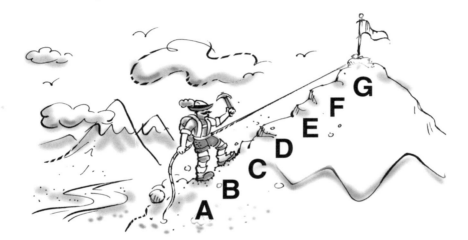

More Minor Scales To Explore

1. The third note in the F harmonic minor scale is ____. _____

2. The sixth note in the *ascending* D melodic minor scale is ____. _____

3. All natural minor scales follow the pattern of W, ___, ___, W, H, ___, W. _____

4. The key signature of ____ minor has 4 sharps. _____

5. The key signature of ____ minor has 6 flats. _____

6. The C minor key signature has 3 _____. _____

Your Total Points Are : _____
(perfect score is 24)

FF1230

Hearing Harmonic Minor Scales

Your teacher will play one mistake in each harmonic minor scale below.
Circle the note where you hear a mistake.
Hint: You may wish to point to each note as your teacher plays.

Teacher: Play the scale correctly first.
        Then play the scale again with one incorrect note.
        Repeat as necessary.

Minor Scale Reference Chart

Note: Fingering for the right hand is above the notes; fingering for the left hand is below the notes.
Play one octave apart when playing scales hands together.

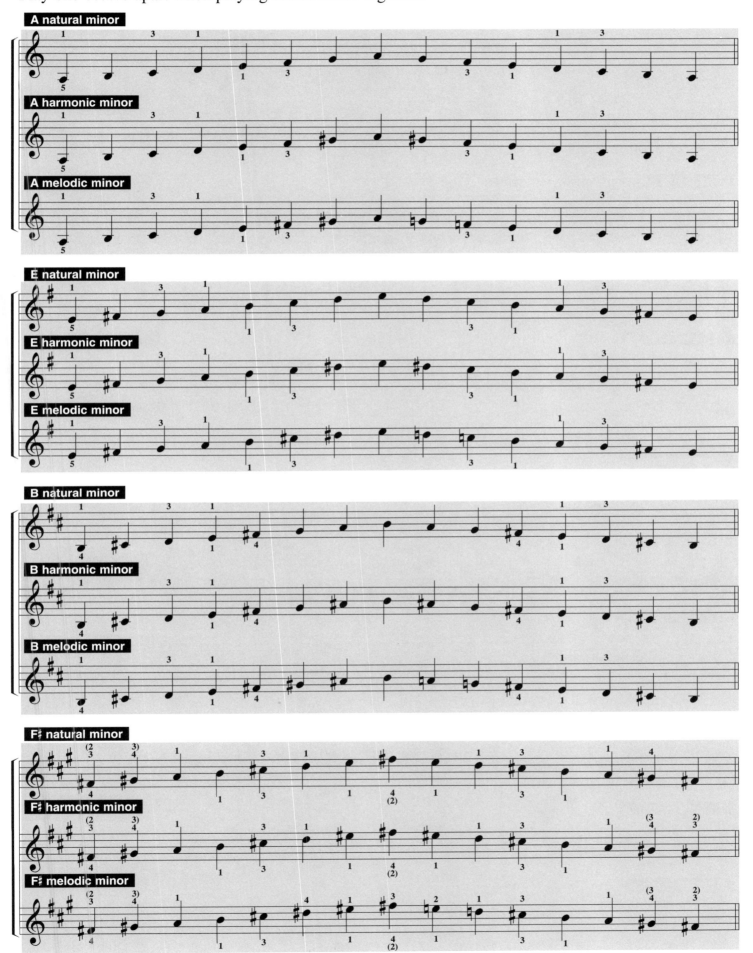

34

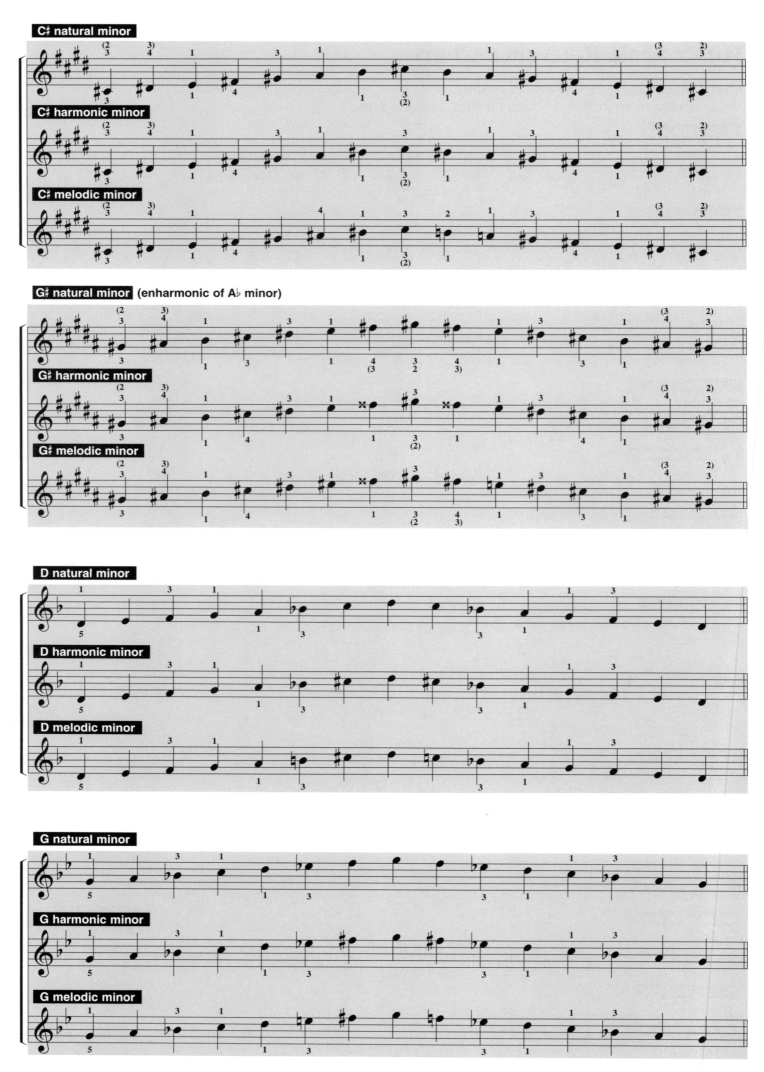

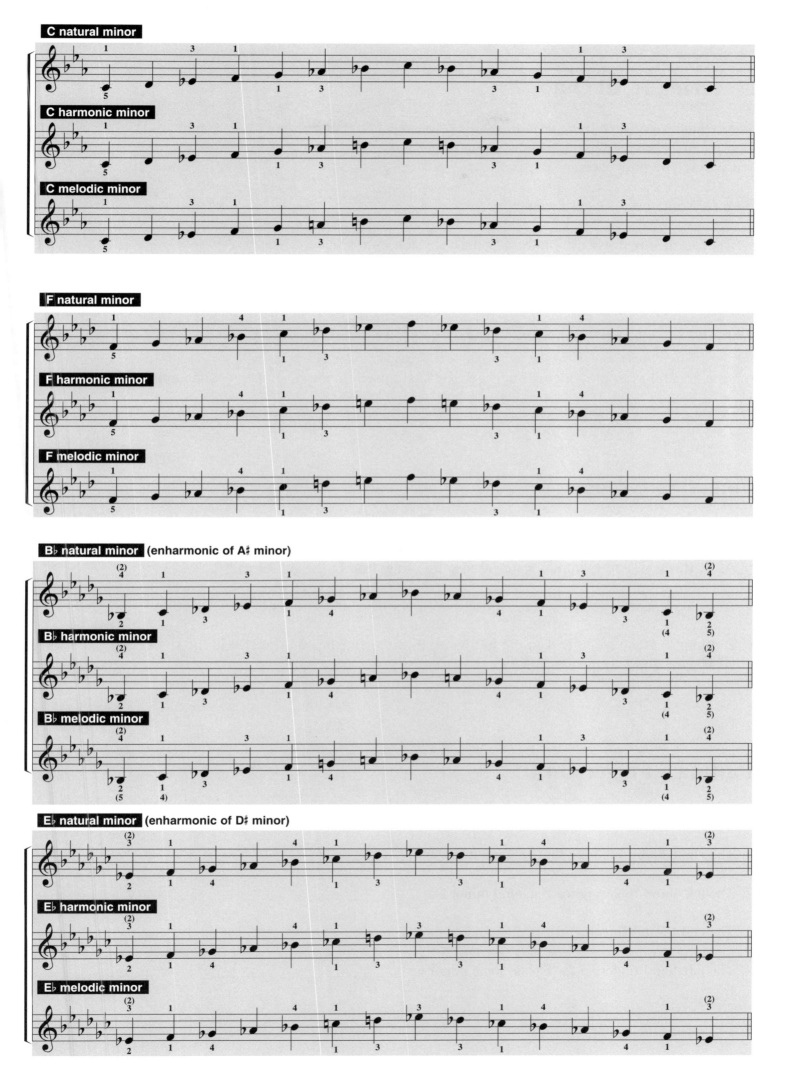

Fingering It All Out

Scale fingering is easy to learn with accurate practice.
That means that you need to use the **same** fingering
every time you play each scale.

Here are some basic fingering rules:

- The fourth finger usually plays only once in each minor scale.
  Memorize where finger 4 goes.

- Thumbs land on the tonic note (scale name) in white key scales.

- If there is a B♭ (A♯) in any scale, the right hand will play it with finger 4.

- As a general rule, the longest fingers (2, 3, 4) are used on the black keys, when applicable.

Fingering Groups

Certain scales "group together" according to their fingering. This makes them easier to learn.

- A, E, B, D, G, and C minor scales all use this fingering in the right hand: 123 12345

- A, E, D, G, and C minor scales all use this fingering in the left hand: 54321 321

- B minor begins on finger 4 in the left hand; F minor finishes on finger 4 in the right hand.
  (**B B**egins and **F F**inishes on 4.)

Putting a Finger On It!

Fill in the blanks below.

1. The **right-hand** fingering for C natural minor is: ___ ___ ___ ___ ___ ___ ___ ___.

2. The **left-hand** fingering for B natural minor is: ___ ___ ___ ___ ___ ___ ___ ___.

3. The **right-hand** fingering for B♭ harmonic minor is: ___ ___ ___ ___ ___ ___ ___ ___ (see p. 35).

4. The **left-hand** fingering for E♭ harmonic minor is: ___ ___ ___ ___ ___ ___ ___ ___ (see p. 35).

Scale Workouts*

These workouts are to be used each day before your scale practice. Just like sports,
scale-playing is athletic and involves many active movements of the fingers, hands, and arms.
Because of this, you need to get in the good habit of warming up before playing. Good luck!

Repeat each workout, playing faster each time. Listen for evenness.

WORKOUT 1 (R.H.)

WORKOUT 2 (L.H.)

*Although the workouts are best suited to the keys of A, E, D, G, and C minor, other scales may be used.
(When using other keys, alter the fingering to fit the scale.)

Review Game

AROUND THE WORLD BY BALLOON

A journey across the minor lands of sharps and flats.

Directions: Beginning at the key of A minor, take a balloon journey to the keys
your teacher chooses. Play the scale(s) for that key. Continue on through
as many sharp or flat lands (keys) as your teacher selects.

Note to Teacher: You may either choose keys in order (A, E, B, etc., or A, D, G, etc.),
or you may select keys in random order (e.g., A, C, F♯, etc.).

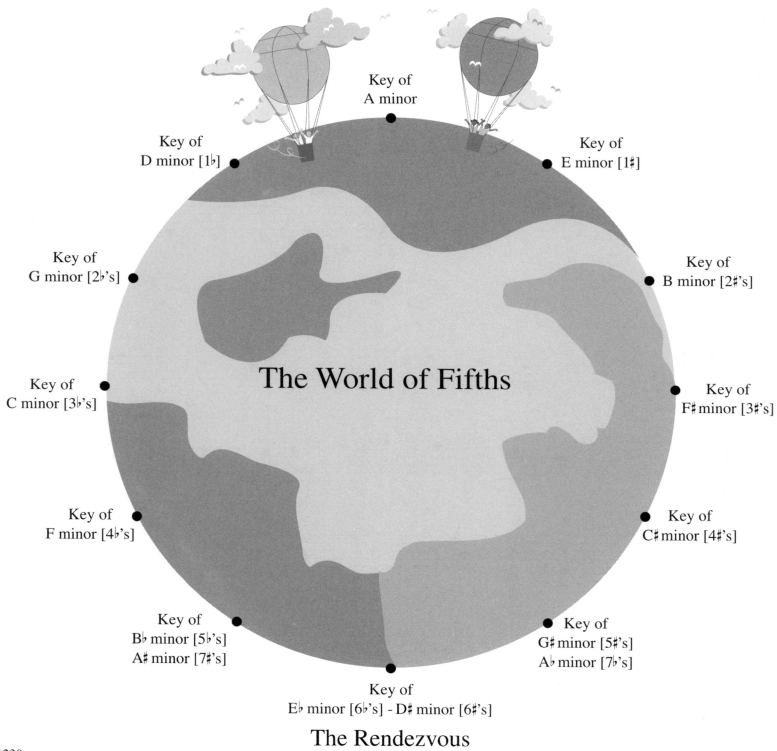

The Rendezvous

Scale Practice Flashcards

(to add variety to practice)

I'M FEELING FLASHY TODAY!

Student Directions:
Cut out the flashcards following the dotted lines, then shuffle them. Draw one from the stack, and follow the practice directions with the scale(s) you have been assigned, or other scales of your choice.

CUT HERE

Play *staccato* **and** *forte (f).*	**Play** *legato* **and** *mezzo piano (mp).*	**Play** *staccato* **and** *piano (p).*
Play your right hand *forte (f),* **and your left hand** *piano (p).*	**Play your right hand** *piano (p),* **and your left hand** *forte (f).*	**Play your right hand** *legato,* **and your left hand** *staccato.*
Play your right hand *staccato,* **and your left hand** *legato.*	*Crescendo* **when going up,** *diminuendo* **when going down.**	**Choose your own dynamic.**
Make your scale sound: happy, gloomy, relaxed (choose one)	**(fill in your choice)**	**(teacher's choice)**

CUT HERE

Play *staccato* and *piano (p)*.	Play *legato* and *mezzo piano (mp)*.	Play *staccato* and *forte (f)*.
Play your right hand *legato*, and your left hand *staccato*.	Play your right hand *piano (p)*, and your left hand *forte (f)*.	Play your right hand *forte (f)*, and your left hand *piano (p)*.
Choose your own dynamic.	*Crescendo* when going up, *diminuendo* when going down.	Play your right hand *staccato*, and your left hand *legato*.
(teacher's choice)	(fill in your choice)	Make your scale sound: happy, gloomy, relaxed (choose one)